# GRACE
## ESSENTIALS

# CHRISTIAN
# FREEDOM

SAMUEL BOLTON

This modernization of an important work by the seventeenth-century Puritan Samuel Bolton addresses certain key questions of the Christian life and answers them in the solidly Biblical fashion we have come to expect of a Puritan author. Especially helpful is the way that he outlines the nature of true Christian freedom: what we have been delivered from and how God expects us to use our freedom. And what is most needed at the present day: he shows us that liberty and obedience are not polar opposites but two sides of the Christian coin.

Michael A. G. Haykin
Professor of Church History and Biblical Spirituality,
The Southern Baptist Theological Seminary,
Louisville, Kentucky

# GRACE
## ESSENTIALS

# CHRISTIAN
# FREEDOM

SAMUEL BOLTON

CHRISTIAN
**HERITAGE**

Unless otherwise indicated Scripture quotations are taken from the *Holy Bible, New International Version*. Copyright © 1973, 1978, 1984 by International Bible Society. Used by permission of Hodder & Stoughton, a member of the Hodder Headline Group. All rights reserved.

Scripture marked NKJV are taken from the *New King James Version*. Copyright © 1982 by Thomas Nelson, Inc. Used by permission. All rights reserved.

A modernised and simplified version of: *The True Bounds of Christian Freedom* by Samuel Bolton (1645)

paperback ISBN 978-1-78191-721-3
epub ISBN 978-1-78191-727-5
mobi ISBN 978-1-78191-724-4

Printed in 2016
in the
Christian Heritage Imprint
by
Christian Focus Publications Ltd,
Geanies House, Fearn, Ross-shire,
IV20 1TW, Scotland, U.K.
www.christianfocus.com
and
Grace Publications Trust
7 Arlington Way
London, EC1R 1XA, England
www.gracepublications.co.uk

Cover design by Pete Barnsley (Creative Hoot)

Printed and bound by
Bell and Bain, Glasgow

# Contents

Preface................................................................ 7

**Chapter 1: What is Christian freedom?**.............. 9

    1.  Freedom from Satan ........................... 11

    2.  Freedom from sin................................ 11

    3.  Freedom from obeying people............ 14

    4.  Freedom from death ......................... 15

    5.  Freedom from the grave .................... 15

**Chapter 2: Freedom from the law**.............. 17

    1.  We are free from the law as a covenant.............. 17

    2.  We are free from the curses of the law .............. 18

    3.  We are free from being accused by the law ......... 20

    4.  We are free from the impossible demands
       of the law........................................... 22

**Chapter 3: Do Christians need to obey God's law?** ...... 27

**Chapter 4: Why should Christians obey God's
              moral law?** .................................. 33

    1.  Jesus said we should obey.................. 33

    2.  The Apostles said we should obey...................... 34

    3.  Answering some objections ............... 35

**Chapter 5: Law and grace**.............................. 41

**Chapter 6: Are Christians free from punishment
when they sin?** ............................................ 47

**Chapter 7: Obedience and freedom** .............................. 51

**Chapter 8: Why do we obey God?** ................................ 55

    1.   Wrong answers to the question ......................... 55

    2.   The true reason why Christians obey God.......... 57

**Chapter 9: Obedience and rewards** .............................. 61

    1.   Material Blessings ............................................. 63

    2.   Spiritual Blessings ............................................. 66

    3.   Eternal Blessings (or Rewards) .......................... 67

**Chapter 10: Can those set free by Christ become
slaves to sin again?** ...................................... 71

    1.   Loss of peace and joy ........................................ 72

    2.   Loss of pleasure in serving God.......................... 73

**Chapter 11: Conclusion** .............................................. 75

    1.   A Word to Non-Christians................................. 75

    2.   A Word to Christians......................................... 77

# Preface

This book is a simplification of *The True Bounds of Christian Freedom* by Samuel Bolton, and is based on the 1996 edition published by the Banner of Truth Trust.

Samuel Bolton was born in London in 1606, and studied at Christ's College, Cambridge. He was a minister in London before returning to Cambridge, first as Master of Christ's College, and then as Vice-Chancellor of Cambridge University. His second book, *The True Bounds of Christian Freedom* was published in 1645.

In this book, Bolton explains and defines what Christian freedom is. This is a subject of great importance for every Christian. What did Jesus mean when He said, 'If the Son sets you free, you will be free indeed' (John 8:36)? Do Christians still have to obey God's law? Are God's law and His grace in conflict with one another? Bolton answers these questions, and many others, in a thoroughly Biblical way.

This book is not simply an academic discussion of the issues; Samuel Bolton constantly reminds his readers of the gospel, and the great transformation that has happened to a person who has trusted in Jesus Christ. Bolton shows us clearly that real Christian obedience comes from a changed heart, and is motivated by love for God. He deals with the practical question of what happens when Christians fall into sin, and encourages us to rely on what Christ has done for us, rather than on our performance.

It is my hope that everyone who reads this book will understand more deeply what it means to have been set free from sin by the work of Jesus Christ, and will be motivated to live for Him and His glory.

Ruth Firth, November 2014.

7

# Chapter 1: What is Christian freedom?

'If the Son sets you free, you will be free indeed'
(John 8:36)

Jesus spoke these words as He was arguing with the Jewish leaders, who were opposing Him. Some of the Jews, John tells us, did believe in Jesus. But there were others who did not want to receive Him, or His teaching, and they say to Jesus, 'We are Abraham's descendants and have never been slaves of anyone. How can you say that we shall be set free?' (John 8:33). This was not true, because many times during their history the Jews had not been a free people (even at the time of Jesus the Jews were not free – they were under Roman rule). Jesus could have reminded them of that, but He doesn't, because He was not talking about political freedom, but about being free from sin, as we see clearly from His answer, 'Everyone who sins is a slave to sin' (v. 34), and in verse 36 He also shows them the way out of this slavery.

That is the context of John 8:36. Now let me look in more detail at the verse itself. There are four points that I want to make:

1. We see a positive quality – freedom.

2. This freedom is described as being *real*, or *true* freedom.

3. We see who has this freedom – those who believe in Jesus.

4. We see who makes us free – Jesus Christ.

We can make the following conclusions from this:

1. That naturally every person is in a state of slavery.

2. That some people are set free from this slavery.

3. That they are set free by Christ.

4. That they are really and truly free.

We can say all this in one sentence:
'Christ has real freedom, and He brings all true believers into this freedom.'

What kind of freedom are we talking about?
There are different kinds of freedom, for example, political freedom. Jesus is not talking about that in John 8:36. There is also sensual 'freedom', or license. This is what Paul speaks against in Galatians 5:13, 'Do not use your freedom to indulge the sinful nature.' It is a terrible thing when people abuse God's grace, taking the opportunity to sin. We read about such people in Jude, verse 4. Such people are not true children of God.

The freedom that Jesus is talking about is spiritual freedom. Jesus has bought this freedom for us, and we are told to stand firm in this freedom (Gal. 5:1).

What are the characteristics of this freedom?
Let me say three things about this freedom:

1. It is real, not imaginary. Some people think they are free when they are not, but this freedom is real.

2. It is complete freedom. We are set free from everything that we were slaves to: from Satan, from sin, from the law, from God's wrath, from death and from hell. This is true for every believer.

3. It is a permanent freedom. We never go back into slavery. We are now God's children, and will never go back to being slaves.

There are two stages to this freedom. There is the freedom we experience here in this life, and then there is the perfect freedom we will experience in heaven. But the freedom we have now is the beginning of that perfect freedom, and in this book we will try to understand more about what this means for us.

Firstly, let me talk about the *'negative'* aspects of our freedom as believers. By this I mean what we are set free *from*.

### 1. Freedom from Satan
It is clear that Jesus has delivered us from Satan, as it says in Hebrews 2:14-15, 'he [Christ] too shared in their humanity so that by his death he might destroy him who holds the power of death—that is, the devil—and free those who all their lives were held in slavery by their fear of death.' By His mighty hand Jesus has rescued us from Satan, just as the Israelites were rescued out of Egypt.

### 2. Freedom from sin
By this I mean that we are free from the guilt of sin, we are washed clean from the pollution of sin, and we are no longer under the controlling power of sin. We are free from God's anger and condemnation. Jesus has taken these on Himself, and has paid for our sin. None of our sins can ever condemn

us, or put us under God's anger or God's curse. 'Therefore, there is now no condemnation for those who are in Christ Jesus' (Rom. 8:1).

This is what God has done, 'the LORD has laid on him the iniquity of us all' (Isa. 53:6). Jesus has taken all our sin, and has fully paid our debt. His resurrection proves that He did so, as Paul makes clear in Romans 8:33-34, 'Who will bring any charge against those whom God has chosen? It is God who justifies. Who is he that condemns? Christ Jesus, who died—more than that, who was raised to life—is at the right hand of God, and is also interceding for us.' None of our sins will ever condemn us.

It is also true to say that none of our sins will ever bring upon us the anger of God and its consequences. We are free from the misery and the punishments which accompany God's anger at sin. God's attitude towards us now is one of constant mercy. None of God's anger will touch us.

Yes, God does discipline us when we sin. But there is an enormous difference between this, and experiencing God's anger. We have a different relationship with God now, and He has a different purpose in mind when He disciplines believers.

God never punishes us or brings difficulties into our lives as a way of 'making us pay' for our sin. This is impossible, because we know that Jesus has paid absolutely everything! When God does discipline us, it is like giving a sick person medicine. He does it to heal us, and make us better. This is not true for ungodly people – God punishes them as a holy Judge, not as a loving Father.

Everything God does to His people is motivated by His love for them. He disciplines them in love, and only for their good. This is not true for unbelievers. They are still under the anger and curse of God and He cannot forget their sin.

We are also free from the controlling power of sin. 'For sin shall not be your master' (Rom. 6:14). Why not? 'Because you are not under law, but under grace.' When we were still under law, then sin was in control – and we were content for sin to control us. We went along with sin, just like a boat floats in the direction that the river flows. We also actively sinned personally, as our desires motivated us to do so. Now, however, Christ has set us free from the controlling power of sin.

However, we still have sin living in us, and this gives us much trouble and sadness. Sin can still cause disruption and harm, just as a defeated enemy often goes on fighting even after it is clear that he cannot win. A godly person can be more troubled by sin (even though it no longer controls him) than he was before he became a Christian. But the difference is this: sin may win a temporary victory, but sin is no longer in control. Sin is no longer king in the heart of a believer. The reign of sin is over, and the believer will never again be happy for sin to rule over him.

Augustine[1] describes four conditions that a person can be in regarding sin:

1. Before he knows the law he doesn't fight against sin.

2. Under the law he fights against sin, but fails to defeat it.

3. Under grace he fights against sin and wins.

4. In heaven he has no more fight, only the enjoyment of victory.

What a wonderful position we are in as believers! Other people are under the control of sin, dictated to by their desires and passions, powerless against temptation. But we are not under

---

[1] Augustine of Hippo (354-430) became a prominent figure in the development of Western Christian theology, and a great defender of the sovereign grace of God in our salvation and in the living of the Christian life.

the controlling power of sin, we no longer enjoy sinning. Sin may win some victories over us, but it is no longer our master. Sin is dying more and more in us. On the cross Jesus fatally wounded sin, and from that moment it has been gradually dying. God has chosen to kill sin gradually, and one of the reasons for this is so that we will learn to rely on God daily for the strength to put sin to death in our lives.

### 3. Freedom from obeying people
The Bible seems to say in some places that we must obey men, and in other places that we must not. How do we understand this?

1. The Bible teaches that we should obey the laws of our country, unless we cannot do so without breaking God's law. That is how we should understand verses such as these:

- 'Everyone must submit himself to the governing authorities, for there is no authority except that which God has established. The authorities that exist have been established by God' (Rom. 13:1).

- 'Submit yourselves for the Lord's sake to every authority instituted among men: whether to the king as the supreme authority, or to governors, who are sent by him to punish those who do wrong and to commend those who do right. For it is God's will that by doing good you should silence the ignorant talk of foolish men' (1 Pet. 2:13-15).

2. The Bible also teaches that in spiritual things we have only one authority over us, and that is God Himself:

- 'And do not call anyone on earth "father," for you have one Father, and he is in heaven. Nor are you to be called "teacher", for you have one Teacher, the Christ' (Matt. 23:9-10).

- 'You were bought at a price; do not become slaves of men' (1 Cor. 7:23).

There is only one master we should obey in spiritual matters, and He is in heaven. We must not allow any other person to rule over our conscience, and we should not obey anyone in the absolute sense in which we obey Jesus Christ. This is what it means to be free from obeying men.

### 4. Freedom from death

By this I mean that the believer is freed from death as a curse. For the believer death is now called 'sleep', and it is not something to be afraid of. The believer also knows that he will not die until it is God's time, and therefore the right time, for him to die.

### 5. Freedom from the grave

This is actually part of the freedom we will enjoy in heaven. Although after death our bodies return to dust, those bodies will be raised to life again, and they will be perfect, glorious bodies, free from sickness and all imperfections, which will never die again. It will be the same body we had before, but made glorious, and our souls will be reunited with it. This is a mystery no-one can understand, but the Bible says it is so: 'I myself will see him with my own eyes—I, and not another. How my heart yearns within me!' (Job 19:27).

So far I have only spoken about the 'negative' side of freedom, or what we are freed *from*. Briefly let me say something about the 'positive' side of our freedom, or what we are freed *to*. This is not a complete list.

15

1. We are freed from a state of being under God's anger into a state of knowing God's mercy and favour (Eph. 2:1-10).

2. We are freed from a state of condemnation into a state of justification (Rom. 8:1).

3. We are freed from being God's enemies and have become His friends (Col. 1:21-22).

4. We are freed from being dead and are made alive (Eph. 2:1-5).

5. We are freed from sin to serve God (Luke 1:74). God paid our debt of sin so that we would be free to serve Him. If we don't realise that serving God is actually being free, then we also don't understand that sin is slavery. This means that we are still not really free.

6. We are freed from a spirit of slavery and given a spirit of sonship. Jesus Christ has redeemed us and made us sons of God. Now we serve God not out of fear, but out of love. Now we have a new nature, and new desires. Just as God's love for us motivated Him to save us, so our love for God motivates us to obey Him.

7. We are freed from death and hell, and brought to life and glory. Heaven is our inheritance, a place is being prepared there for us, and we are being prepared for it (Rom. 9:23). This is called the 'glorious freedom of the children of God' (Rom. 8:21). It is impossible for us fully to understand what this means (1 Cor. 2:9), but is described in the Bible as glory, joy, the Master's joy, the Father's house, the kingdom of glory, eternal life, eternal glory. This is the glorious freedom of the children of God!

# Chapter 2: Freedom from the law

Part of the freedom that Jesus gives us is freedom from the law. 'But now, by dying to what once bound us, we have been released from the law so that we serve in the new way of the Spirit, and not in the old way of the written code' (Rom. 7:6). 'For through the law I died to the law so that I might live for God' (Gal. 2:19).

We are freed from the ceremonial law, which was a heavy burden, as we clearly see from Acts 15:10. But this is only a small part of what freedom from the law means. I will now explain what else is included in this freedom from the law.

## 1. We are free from the law as a covenant

There are two ways that the Bible talks about the purpose of God's law. The first way sees the law as a contract we need to keep in order to earn, or deserve, life. When we read Bible passages that talk about the law no longer being binding to us as believers we need to understand these passages in this first sense, that we no longer need to keep the law to earn life. In fact we no longer expect to earn anything by keeping the law – we now look to gain life and everything else in Christ. The apostle Paul knew this to be true. There was a time in his life when he hoped to earn life by keeping the law, but he realised instead that the law killed him – because he could not keep it. 'Once I was alive apart from law; but when the commandment came, sin sprang to life and I died. I found that the very commandment that was intended to bring life actually brought death' (Rom. 7:9-10). Later in his life he says, 'For through the law I died to the law so that I might live for God' (Gal. 2:19). Now the law as a covenant has absolutely nothing to do with the believer, because he has died to the law.

The second way the Bible talks about God's law is that it shows us how Christians should live. When we read about the law still being important for believers, we need to understand it in this sense – as a rule of how to live.

### 2. We are free from the curses of the law

For those who are under the law as a covenant, the law requires the following: either you must perfectly keep all the law all the time, or you must pay the cost of failing to keep the law. You must either obey totally, or experience the curses for disobedience. Everyone who doesn't believe in Jesus is in this unhappy position, 'Whoever does not believe stands condemned already' (John 3:18) and 'God's wrath remains on him' (John 3:36).

But believers are free from keeping the law as a covenant in order to earn life. And because we are free from the law as a covenant, we are also free from the curses of the law. The law – and how well we keep it – now has no effect on our eternal state before God. As Paul says in Romans 8:1, 'Therefore, there is now no condemnation for those who are in Christ Jesus.'

We cannot keep the law because we are sinners. So the law cannot save us, it can only condemn us. 'All who rely on observing the law are under a curse, for it is written: "Cursed is everyone who does not continue to do everything written in the Book of the Law"' (Gal. 3:10).

Jesus Christ has bought freedom for everyone who is in Him. He has freed us from the curses of the law, by taking the curses for us, 'Christ redeemed us from the curse of the law by becoming a curse for us, for it is written: "Cursed is everyone who is hung on a tree"' (Gal. 3:13). The law cannot condemn the believer, because Christ has completely kept and fulfilled the law for him.

This privilege belongs to the believer forever; even though a believer may fall into sin, he does not come under the curse of the law, because in Jesus he has been set free from the law. As it says in Colossians 2:14, God 'cancelled the written code [the law], with its regulations, that was against us and stood opposed to us; he took it away, nailing it to the cross.' Notice what this verse actually says; first, that God 'cancelled' the law, and then that He 'took it away', and finally that He 'nailed it to the cross'. From this we should understand that there is no possibility of a believer ever again being condemned by the law.

So the law cannot condemn believers because they are in Jesus, and Jesus has completely fulfilled the law for them. They are not under the authority of the law to judge them, because they have asked for God's mercy. We see this in the parable of the Pharisee and the tax collector (Luke 18). The tax collector asks God for mercy, 'God, have mercy on me, a sinner' (Luke 18:13), and he goes home justified, not condemned. Why was his prayer answered? Because he was really humbled by his sinfulness – he knew he was not worthy to come to God, but stood at a distance, not even daring to look up (v. 13). He knew that there was nothing he could do to be right with God, and that he needed God's mercy.

19

A person needs to see their sinfulness before they will call on God for mercy. When we see that we are totally unable to keep the law, then we realise that our only hope is mercy, and we ask God to be merciful. When we do this, then God takes us out of the reach of the law, and we cannot be condemned. We have found safety in Jesus.

It is a wonderful position to be in, to be free from the curses of the law, and to have the promises and blessings of Christ instead. It is a wonderful mercy of God, that none of His anger at sin will now fall on us.

### 3. We are free from being accused by the law

Satan is very active in accusing God's people; he is called 'the accuser of our brothers, who accuses them before our God day and night' (Rev. 12:10). Satan is always accusing us of our sin, as we see him doing to Joshua (Zech. 3:1-4). He is the one who tempts us to sin, and as soon as we have sinned, he is the one who says that we are guilty.

Satan also accuses us before God in the same way as he did with Job – that is, he accuses our motives. He accused Job of serving God in order to get material blessings from Him.

Sometimes Satan also makes accusations against God, as he did with Adam and Eve, when he accused God of not wanting Adam and Eve to be wise like Him (Gen. 3:5). Satan also encourages people to sin by telling them that God will forgive them, and then he makes them afraid by telling them that if they have sinned, there is no hope of forgiveness for them.

But whatever accusations Satan may make, he has no power to condemn. We see this again in the case of Joshua (Zech. 3). Even though Satan's accusation against Joshua was true – Joshua was wearing dirty clothes – God did not allow it, 'The LORD rebuke you, Satan! ... Is not this man a burning stick snatched from the fire?' (Zech. 3:2).

As well as Satan, wicked people may also accuse God's people. Sometimes they accuse us for sins that we have done, which shows their lack of love in not forgetting what God has forgiven. At other times they may accuse us of sins we have not committed, as Potiphar's wife did with Joseph (Gen. 39:17). But they cannot condemn us.

Our conscience may also accuse us. We need to listen to our conscience when it accuses us of actual sin, and we see many examples of this in the Bible (e.g. David, after he had made a census of the people; Joseph's brothers after they had sold him into slavery). We can only be sure that we are guilty of sin if our conscience agrees with the word of God. If our conscience is calling something a sin when God's word does not, then we must not listen to it. Our conscience is not perfect. At other times our conscience can remind us of old sins, which we have already confessed to God. When this happens, we are not to listen to our conscience. God has not condemned us for these sins, and we should not allow our conscience to condemn us, either.

So there are many who accuse us – Satan, wicked people, our own conscience, and finally, the law itself. Before we believed in Jesus, the law had the power to accuse us of sin, and not only to accuse, but to condemn us. But now that we are in Christ, the law cannot accuse us of sins we committed before we became Christians, because we have been forgiven. Neither can the law accuse us of the sins we commit after we become Christians, because we are not 'under law' any more. Where Paul asks in Romans 8:33, 'Who will bring any charge against those whom God has chosen?' we could also understand this to mean, 'Who shall call God's people into court?' We are no longer judged by the court of the law, but by the court of the Gospel. This actually makes us more sorry for our sin, and leads us quickly to repent of it.

The law can show a Christian that he has sinned, but the law cannot condemn him for that sin. The law may, however, accuse a Christian of sin in order to humble him and to help him grow in holiness. All unbelievers are accused by the law and are also condemned by it. For believers, the law can only help them to grow in holiness.

You may be wondering how the law can have any place in the life of a Christian, as I have said that Christians are not under the law. I will answer briefly for now: Christians are not under the law's curses, but we are under its commands. In other words, the law shows Christians how we should live, but does not judge us. The law is now our helper; it shows us what sin is, so that we can repent of it and grow in holiness. The law still has a place in the life of a believer; the law shows us how we may please God, after we have been justified by faith in Jesus. We now keep God's law as *sons*, not as slaves, and there is a great difference between these two conditions. I will talk more on this subject later.

### 4. We are free from the impossible demands of the law
By this I do not mean that the law has somehow been changed for Christians. So what do I mean?

*Firstly* this: that the law commanded us to do things that were not only difficult for us to do, they were impossible. And the law could not give us any help, either. It is like Pharaoh, who commanded the Israelites to make bricks, but would not give them any straw to make the bricks with (Exod. 5:10-11), or like the Pharisees, who put heavy burdens on the people, but did not help them to carry those burdens (Matt. 23:4).

But now, in the Gospel, we are freed from impossibilities. Everything is possible now, because God is working for us and in us. Chrysostom[2] praised God for the fact that what God demanded from him, God also gave him. The works the Gospel commands are actually greater than anything the law requires, as the Gospel commands us to believe, which is a greater work than all the works of the law. But God gives us the strength to believe, and Jesus strengthens us. Just as He said, 'Apart from me you can do nothing' (John 15:5), so it is also true that 'I can do everything through him who gives me strength' (Phil. 4:13). A weak Christian with a strong Jesus can do anything. Nothing will be too hard for the person who has the strength of Christ and the Spirit of Christ working with him.

The Gospel includes in itself the power to do what it commands us to do. For example, in Romans 6:12 we have a command, 'Do not let sin reign in your mortal body.' Then in verse 14 we have a promise, 'For sin shall not be your master, because you are not under law, but under grace.' In other words, 'Now you are under grace, you will have the power to put sin to death.'

*Secondly*, the law demanded that each person keep the law himself – no-one else could do it for him. We are free from this demand, and God accepts the work of Jesus in our place. We owed God two debts – we needed to pay for our sin, and we needed to completely obey Him. Jesus has done both those things for us. He has paid for all our sin, and He has completely kept God's law for us, so that we are described as being given 'fullness' [or perfection] in Him (Col. 2:10).

---

[2] John Chrysostom (c.347-407) bishop of Constantinople and influential theologian and Bible teacher.

*Thirdly*, the law demanded that we keep all of it, all the time, absolutely, without a single failure. Anyone who failed to do this was condemned. 'All who rely on observing the law are under a curse, for it is written: "Cursed is everyone who does not continue to do everything written in the Book of the Law"' (Gal. 3:10). However hard a person tried to keep the law, however much he or she *wanted* to keep the law – this made no difference. The smallest failure meant complete failure. Nothing could change that – not even repentance, not praying, not trying harder in the future. One single failure, and all was lost.

The Gospel accepts repentance, but the law does not. The law required perfect obedience, all the time. God has freed the believer from this. Instead of complete obedience, God accepts our desire to obey Him, even though we fail at times. We may fail to keep God's law, but God looks at our desires, and is pleased with our efforts to keep His law, even though we fail. In the Gospel God accepts our sincere efforts instead of demanding perfect performance from us.

Adam did not obey God because he did not want to. That is no longer true of believers. We want to obey God, but we lack the power. Our will is not perfect – we don't *always* want to do what is right, but generally we fail to obey God due to a lack of strength, not because we don't want to obey Him. This is what Paul says in Romans 7:18, 'I have the desire to do what is good, but I cannot carry it out.' God is merciful towards people like that, who cannot keep His law. He is not merciful towards those who do not want to keep His law. To God, being weak is very different from being wicked. In the Gospel God sees the weakness of believers, and our weakness makes Him have pity on us. Under the law, a person's sin makes him the object of God's hatred, but under the Gospel, a person's sin makes him the object of God's pity.

*Fourthly*, the law declared terrible punishment if we failed to keep it. In other words, the law used fear of punishment to motivate us to obedience. The Gospel is completely different; it attracts us with a message of love and mercy, and motivates us to obey out of love, not out of fear. 'Therefore, I urge you, brothers, in view of God's mercy, to offer your bodies as living sacrifices' (Rom. 12:1). 'For Christ's love compels us' (2 Cor. 5:14). In the Gospel the spirit is not one of slavery and fear, but of power and love (Rom. 8:15; 2 Tim. 1:7). There is nothing more powerful than love. Things that are usually impossible for us to do become possible for us if we do them for someone we love. This is how we should understand Jesus' words in Matthew 11:30, 'My yoke is easy and my burden is light.' Where there are difficulties, love overcomes them. Jacob served Laban for seven years so that he could marry Rachel, and the time 'seemed like only a few days to him because of his love for her' (Gen. 29:20). God gives a spirit of love to His children, and that love is what motivates them to serve Him. This spirit of love means that they delight in and enjoy doing things which otherwise would be burdens to them.

What a wonderful privilege believers have. God has set us free from the impossible demands of the law.

# Chapter 3: Do Christians need to obey God's law?

We can ask the same question like this, 'If Jesus has set us free, do we still need to obey God's law?'

Before we go further, let us make clear what we mean when we talk about God's law. God's law can basically be thought of as three kinds of laws: ceremonial, judicial and moral. I will explain the differences between these three later.

When we see the word 'law' used in the Bible, we need to decide what meaning of the word is being used. There a number of different ways the word 'law' is used, and I will mention the main ones:

i) The word *law* can mean the Old Testament, as for example in John 12:34, where the people say, 'We have heard from the Law that the Christ will remain for ever.' In John 15:25 Jesus quotes Psalm 35 when He says, 'But this is to fulfil what is written in their Law: "They hated me without reason."'

ii) *Law* can mean the first 5 books of the Bible, as for example in John 1:45, where Philip tells Nathaniel, 'We have found the one Moses wrote about in the Law, and about whom the prophets also wrote.' Jesus uses it in the same sense in Luke 24:44, 'Everything must be fulfilled that is written about me in the Law of Moses, the Prophets and the Psalms.'

iii) The word *law* can simply mean the moral law of God, that is, the 10 commandments. This is how it is used in Romans 7:7,14,21.

iv) It can mean the ceremonial law, as in Luke 16:16, where Jesus says: 'The Law and the Prophets were proclaimed until John' [the Baptist].

v) It can mean all of God's laws, ceremonial, judicial and moral. This is the case in John 1:17: 'For the law was given through Moses; grace and truth came through Jesus Christ.' Grace replaced the moral law and truth replaced the ceremonial.

The *ceremonial* laws were designed to point the Jewish people to their need of a Saviour. Now that He has come, these laws are no longer necessary.

The *judicial* laws had three main purposes. One was to show the Israelites how they should govern themselves, another was to make them different from the people around them, and the third was to give them a picture of what Christ's government would be like in the future.

So that leaves the third kind of law the Bible talks about – God's *moral* law, which is given in the 10 commandments and how these commandments are explained in more detail in other parts of the Bible. Some people say that Christians don't have to keep these laws, because they are free from the law. Here are some of the Bible verses which talk about Christians being free from God's moral law:

**Romans 7:1-2 and 6-7,** 'Do you not know, brothers—for I am speaking to men who know the law—that the law has authority over a man only as long as he lives? For example, by law a married woman is bound to her husband as long as he is alive, but if her husband dies, she is released from the law of marriage.' When we read further, it is clear (in verse 7) that Paul is talking about God's moral law, and he clearly says in verse 6 that believers are free from this law, 'We have been released from the law' (Rom. 7:6). 'I would not have known what coveting really was if the law had not said, "Do not covet"' (Rom. 7:7).

**Romans 6:14**, 'For sin shall not be your master, because you are not under law, but under grace.'

**Galatians 4:4-5**, 'But when the time had fully come, God sent his Son, born of a woman, born under law, to redeem those under law, that we might receive the full rights of sons.'

**Romans 8:2**, 'Through Christ Jesus the law of the Spirit of life set me free from the law of sin and death.'

**Galatians 5:18**, 'But if you are led by the Spirit, you are not under law.'

**Romans 10:4**, 'Christ is the end of the law so that there may be righteousness for everyone who believes.'

**1 Timothy 1:8-9**, 'We know that the law is good if one uses it properly. We also know that law is made not for the righteous but for lawbreakers and rebels, the ungodly and sinful, the unholy and irreligious…'

So there seems to be a strong argument for saying that the law is no longer in force for believers – they are dead to the law, free from the law and no longer under the law. We will look at what these verses mean later. For now, I simply quote them.

Other people say that Christians must keep these laws, and there are verses in the Bible which also say that. For example:

**Romans 3:31**, 'Do we, then, nullify the law by this faith? Not at all! Rather, we uphold the law.'

**Matthew 5:17-18**, 'Do not think that I have come to abolish the Law or the Prophets; I have not come to abolish them but to fulfil them. I tell you the truth, until heaven and earth disappear, not the smallest letter, not the least stroke of a pen, will by any means disappear from the Law until everything is accomplished.'

We know that the Bible always speaks the truth, so we need to think carefully about this subject. Everyone agrees that we are set free from the curses and punishments that went with the law, but we still need to answer the question, 'Is the moral law something that Christians must obey today?'

Some Christians say that, since Jesus has come, we no longer need to obey the moral law. I cannot agree with this, and I will explain why in the next chapter.

There are two other views amongst Christians; one is that we are bound to obey the moral law of the Old Testament, and the other view is that we are to obey the commands Jesus gave us, for example, 'A new command I give you: Love one another. As I have loved you, so you must love one another' (John 13:34).

In actual fact, whether you take the 10 commandments as your guide for living, or look at the commands of Jesus, you will find the same teachings. This is how it should be, as the moral standards of God's law cannot change. Good and evil do not change, so neither does God's law, which shows us what is good and what is evil. The moral law shows us what pleases God – that we should love Him, and love our neighbours. Just as God Himself does not change, what pleases Him also does not change. We understand that the law shows us the will of God, and so we want to obey it – but not because we expect to get life and blessing from keeping it, or are afraid that we will be punished if we fail to do so.

For Christians, the law has no power either to declare us righteous or to condemn us. Its purpose now is to direct our lives, to show us how to live. We are no longer under the curse of the law, but we should still obey its commands. If we say we are free from obedience, we are actually servants of sin.

To Christians who think that we do not need to obey God's moral law, I will make two points.

1. The moral law is still the rule of how a Christian should live.

2. God's law is not in conflict with God's grace.

I will look at these points in detail in the next two chapters.

## Chapter 4: Why should Christians obey God's moral law?

### 1. Jesus said we should obey

This is historically the way Christian churches have understood the matter, but more importantly it is the teaching of the New Testament. For example, the words of Jesus in Matthew 5:17- 18, 'Do not think that I have come to abolish the Law or the Prophets; I have not come to abolish them but to fulfil them. I tell you the truth, until heaven and earth disappear, not the smallest letter, not the least stroke of a pen, will by any means disappear from the Law until everything is accomplished.'

Jesus clearly taught that the law remains in force, 'Anyone who breaks one of the least of these commandments and teaches others to do the same will be called least in the kingdom of heaven, but whoever practises and teaches these commands will be called great in the kingdom of heaven' (Matt. 5:19).

These verses seem to make clear that we should keep the law, but not all Christians agree on this. Some say that Jesus has fulfilled the law, and has therefore made it unnecessary for us to keep it. They use what Paul says in Romans 10:4, 'Christ is the end of the law so that there may be righteousness for everyone who believes.' We must understand this verse correctly. Paul does not mean that Christ is the end of the law because He abolished, or got rid of it. Jesus is the 'end of the law' in the sense that He completely fulfilled, or perfectly kept it.

In the verses from Matthew 5, Jesus uses stronger language than the Pharisees did. Jesus strengthened the law in these verses. Neither Jesus nor the apostles ever said that the law was no longer in force. In fact, they made many statements which show that for them God's law was a rule of life.

## 2. The Apostles said we should obey

For example:

- *The apostle Paul* said the following, 'we uphold the law' (Rom. 3:31), 'the law is holy, and the commandment is holy, righteous and good' (Rom. 7:12), 'in my inner being I delight in God's law' (Rom. 7:22) and 'I myself in my mind am a slave to God's law' (Rom. 7:25).

- *James* says, 'If you really keep the royal law found in Scripture, "Love your neighbour as yourself," you are doing right' (James 2:8).

- And *the apostle John* says, 'The man who says, "I know him," but does not do what he commands is a liar, and the truth is not in him' (1 John 2:4). And again, 'Everyone who sins breaks the law; in fact, sin is lawlessness' (1 John 3:4).

Christians who say that we do not have to obey the law any longer need to show from the Bible where this change took place. At what point are we taught that the law is no longer a rule of how to live?

It is absolutely impossible to prove from the New Testament that the law no longer applies to Christians. Jesus and His apostles commanded the same things that the law commanded, and did not allow the same things that the law did not allow.

In their writings the apostles tell Christians to do the things that the law commands. For example, Romans 12:19, 'Do not take revenge, my friends, but leave room for God's wrath, for it is written: "It is mine to avenge; I will repay," says the Lord.' Here Paul quotes from Deuteronomy 32:35, the Old Testament law. He does the same in Romans 13:8-10, 'Let no debt remain outstanding, except the continuing debt to love one another, for he who loves his fellow-man has fulfilled the law. The commandments, "Do not commit adultery," "Do not murder," "Do not steal," "Do not covet," and whatever other commandment there may be, are summed up in this one rule: "Love your neighbour as yourself." Love does no harm to its neighbour. Therefore love is the fulfilment of the law.'

Another example is Ephesians 6:1-3, 'Children, obey your parents in the Lord, for this is right. "Honour your father and mother" – which is the first commandment with a promise –"that it may go well with you and that you may enjoy long life on the earth."'

### 3. Answering some objections

Some people, in response to this, say, 'Yes, the law shows us how we should live, but we are free, and so can choose whether to obey it or not.' In answer I would say, 'How can it be a law, then, if we can choose whether or not to obey it?'

We do not have to keep the law in order to be saved, but the law shows us how to please God. It is our duty to keep God's law, as we see in Luke 17:10, 'So you also, when you have done everything you were told to do, should say, "We are unworthy servants; we have only done our duty."'

If we keep God's law, we have a clear conscience, and if we break it, we have a guilty conscience, even as Christians. We are not free to decide whether or not to keep God's law, because 'sin is lawlessness' (1 John 3:4). If it is sin to break the law, how can we say that Christians do not need to keep it?

At this point some people fall into a most serious error, by claiming that Christians don't need the law because they cannot sin. Here they totally contradict the Bible, 'If we claim to be without sin, we deceive ourselves and the truth is not in us' (1 John 1:8). 'If we claim we have not sinned, we make him [God] out to be a liar and his word has no place in our lives' (1 John 1:10).

Then these people say, 'God doesn't look at the sins Christians commit. He accepts us in Jesus, and is pleased with us no matter what we do.'

Let me answer this by making the following points:

i) Perfect good – that is, God – must always hate evil. God always hates sin, no matter who commits it. The nearer the evil is to Him, the more He hates it. God is displeased by a Christian's sin, even though He forgives us.

ii) God has not changed His standards; His moral law is still the same, and breaking it is still sin. Therefore, it cannot be right for Christians to sin.

iii) God's law shows us what holiness looks like, and God desires His children to be holy, like Him. It should be our desire, too, even though we will fall short.

iv) Being 'free in Christ' cannot mean being free from the law, because the law is holy, right and good. How can

being free from something which is holy be real freedom? Obeying the law is part of our Christian freedom,
as we see in Luke 1:74-75 Jesus came, 'to rescue us from
the hand of our enemies, and to enable us to serve him
without fear in holiness and righteousness before him all
our days.'

Obedience is important!

What I have said should make it very clear that as Reformed
Christians we do not believe or teach that Christians can live
any way they like. We teach that we must obey the law of God,
but not in order to be saved. The Catholic Church teaches
that a person must obey in order to be justified. Reformed
churches teach that a person must be justified *before* he can
obey God's law. We believe that obedience is the fruit of
justification.

You do not know Christ if you do not live in obedience
to God's law. You do not know Christ if you think that your
obedience makes God accept you. It is very difficult to live in
obedience to God's law without starting to think that your
obedience makes God accept you. All of us very easily fall into
the trap of trying to create our own righteousness, trying to
get into heaven by our own efforts.

There are so many people in the world today who are
relying on their own good works, rather than on Jesus. Instead
of trying to earn their salvation, they need to believe in Him.
Christians can live like this, too – that's why we have so many
'ups and downs' in our Christian lives; we rely too much on
our performance, and therefore become so easily discouraged
by our failures. Actually what we should do is this: when
we fail, we should remember what Jesus has done for us;
and when we 'succeed', we should remember that this too
depends on Jesus.

People who are antinomians ('antinomian' means 'against law') say that the law has no part to play in a Christian's sanctification[3]; we believe that Christians are free from the curses of the law, but not from its guidance and commands. The law of God shows sinners that we need the gospel to be saved, and then the gospel tells us to look at the law, where we learn how forgiven sinners should live. Our obedience is simply how we thank God for His free forgiveness.

It is very clear in the Bible that we are saved *so that* we can serve God. For example in the first part of the book of Romans Paul shows clearly that we are justified freely by God's grace. Then he makes this statement, 'Therefore, brothers, we have an obligation' (Rom. 8:12). Christ has paid our debt of sin, and we now owe Him a debt of service. He redeemed us from slavery, and brought us into the freedom to serve Him.

Before we were redeemed, we tried to keep God's law in our own strength, motivated by fear or guilt, trying to earn salvation. Now, we obey in a new way, as God's children. We are motivated by love to God, and obedience is a pleasure to us. Love overcomes difficulties; love makes impossible things easy. Now we obey in the strength of Jesus, because we have fellowship with Him. We can do nothing without Jesus, but everything with Him – this is what He has promised. We also obey with a different aim in mind, one that is not self-serving. We are not trying to earn salvation – we are saved already. We obey God now so that He will be glorified, so that people will see how wonderful the gospel is, and to show our thanks to God.

---

[3] Sanctification, simply put, is growth in likeness to Christ. The NT teaches it is a process, beginning when we are born again by the work of the Holy Spirit, and continuing throughout our earthly lives, in which our obedience cooperates with God's work in us.

As I close this chapter let me say this: be careful to use the law in the right way. When we put obedience and good works in the right place, then the law is holy, right and good for us. But when we think that we earn eternal life by keeping the law, we are actually saying that the life and death of Jesus were unnecessary. Keep things in the right order: first, grace, then the law. Remember Luke 1:74: you were redeemed first, so that *then* you may serve.

Let the mercy you have received motivate you to obey God. Do not abuse His mercy. Jesus has done everything needed for your salvation, and this truth should make you more willing to serve Him, not less. A Christian should never think, 'Jesus has done it all, so I can sit and do nothing' or, 'Jesus died for me, so I don't need to pray very much'. The fact that Jesus did die for you should make you love Him more, and want to live for Him.

It would be even worse if a Christian said, 'God has been merciful to me, so I can continue to sin'. Paul deals with that in Romans 6:1-2, 'What shall we say then? Shall we go on sinning, so that grace may increase? By no means! We died to sin; how can we live in it any longer?'

God's generous mercy calls for a response of whole-hearted obedience. If God had not been merciful to us, where would we be? Let us obey Him because He gave us His Son, because His Son gave Himself for us, and because faith without obedience is dead.

If we do not live to serve God, then what will unbelievers think of the gospel? What impression will they have of Jesus? Will they see how wonderful he is? Will they see how great our God is? We want the world to see that the gospel is glorious – so let us walk in obedience to our God!

## Chapter 5: Law and grace

In this chapter I will explain that the law of God is not in conflict with the grace of God, and that actually God's law can help us understand God's grace better.

Let me begin by listing the reasons why God gave us His law.

### 1. To set boundaries so that sin would not become completely out of control.

In the law we see what is right and wrong, and also that God is angry at sin, and will punish everyone who breaks His law. This fear of punishment means that people do not do all the evil things they want to, and so the world is not as terrible a place as it could be. If God had not given us the law, then everyone would treat his brother like Cain treated Abel; every son would treat his father like Absalom treated David, and every servant would treat his master like Judas treated Christ. We should be so thankful that God has shown us what is right, and that sin will be punished. Otherwise none of us could live in safety – our streets and houses would be full of murder, rape, adultery and so on. If there were no law saying 'Do not murder', every argument would end in someone being killed. If there were no law saying 'Do not steal', then people would simply take whatever they wanted by cheating, lying or by force. God has put limits in place, for our own protection – just as He has done in nature, as He set limits for the sea so that it does not flood the earth.

## 2. To show us that we are sinners.

As the apostle Paul says in Romans 7:7, 'Is the law sin? Certainly not! Indeed I would not have known what sin was except through the law. For I would not have known what coveting really was if the law had not said, "Do not covet."' Another purpose of God's law is to show us that we are sinners, and so make us see our need of a Saviour. This is why God gave the law *after* He gave the promise of a Saviour. It was to make people value that promise, because they could see that they needed a Saviour.

## 3. To humble us.

This follows from the second point – God gave us His law to speak to our conscience, so that we would see that we are guilty. This is what Paul means in Romans 3:19, 'Now we know that whatever the law says, it says to those who are under the law, so that every mouth may be silenced and the whole world held accountable to God.' People were sinners before God gave them His law, but they could more easily ignore the voice of conscience. As Paul says in Romans 5:13-14, 'For before the law was given, sin was in the world. But sin is not taken into account when there is no law. Nevertheless, death reigned from the time of Adam to the time of Moses…' There was just as much sin in the world before God gave the law to Moses, and it was punished with death. But men did not 'take account' of their sin, and so God gave them His law to show them more clearly the danger they were in, and the great need they had of a Saviour. God's law should make us value

His grace more; as we see more of our sinfulness, we are more thankful to God for giving us His Son.

### 4. *To show Christians how to live.*

We looked at this in some detail in chapter 4, so here I will only say that Christians must honour and serve their Creator, and the law shows them how to do so.

### 5. *To show Christians their need of Christ.*

The law shows Christians that we do not honour or serve God as He deserves, and so it shows us our constant need of our Saviour, Jesus. In Him there is grace to cover all our sin and imperfection.

### 6. *To discipline and correct Christians.*

In 2 Timothy 3:16 we read: 'All Scripture is God-breathed and is useful for teaching, rebuking, correcting and training in righteousness'. The law of God is especially useful in rebuking and correcting Christians when we sin, and in encouraging us to obey God.

The reasons God gave us His law are not in conflict with His grace. The following points show us the relationship of God's law and His grace:

- It was because of His grace that God gave us His law – if He had not done so, then this world would be a most dreadful place to live in.

- We also see that God's grace goes further than His law; God's law controls sin to some extent because people are afraid of punishment, but God's grace changes a person's heart. Faith in the Gospel does not only limit sin, it has victory over sin.

- God's law also shows us our need of a Saviour, by showing what sin really is, and how we are all guilty before God. In this way, the law prepares the way for the Gospel, as Paul explains in Galatians 3:23-24, 'Before this faith came, we were held prisoners by the law, locked up until faith should be revealed. So the law was put in charge to lead us to Christ that we might be justified by faith.' If God didn't humble us by giving us the law, we would never come to Christ.

- Once we become Christians, the law is still necessary for us. Although we are now God's children, and love Him from the heart, we need to learn how to show our love for Him. We want to please God, and His law shows us how to do so. It is a light for our feet and a lamp for our path. Our obedience is not the reason that we are accepted by God, but it is how we show our thankfulness to Him because He has accepted us. Remember that God gave the promise of salvation first, and then the law second, which shows us that we do not earn salvation by keeping the law, but we keep the law because we have been saved. We do this in the strength of Christ, not in our own strength.

- It is important to understand that we do not make ourselves holy by obeying the law. The law itself cannot change us, because we need to be changed from the inside. We cannot become holy by doing the things that we read in God's law; we need Jesus Christ Himself to change us from the inside – this is what Paul is talking about in Romans 8:2, 'through Christ Jesus the law of the Spirit of life set me free from the law of sin and death'.

Sometimes we can become confused about the purpose of God's law, especially when we read verses such as Leviticus 18:5, 'Keep my decrees and laws, for the man who obeys them will live by them'. This seems to say that it is possible to be saved by keeping God's law, rather than by God's grace alone, which other verses in the Bible clearly teach, for example Galatians 3:11, 'Clearly no one is justified before God by the law, because, "The righteous will live by faith"', and in Ephesians 2:8-9, 'For it is by grace you have been saved, through faith—and this not from yourselves, it is the gift of God—not by works, so that no-one can boast.'

To help us understand this, we can look at Jesus speaking with the rich young ruler in Matthew 19:16-22. Here the young ruler comes and asks Jesus, 'Teacher, what good thing must I do to get eternal life?' Jesus gives what seems like a strange answer, 'If you want to enter into life, obey the commandments.' Is Jesus saying there is another way to be saved? Other times when He was asked the same question He told people to believe in Him (see John 6:28-29). So what is He doing here? To understand it, we need to see that Jesus was talking to a proud young man, who thought that he had kept God's law, as we see from what he says in verse 20: 'All these I have kept'. So with a person like that, Jesus uses the law to show him that he is not perfect, and cannot keep God's law. Jesus uses the law to humble the proud, so that they might see their need of Him. But to people who already know that they are sinners, Jesus gives this gracious promise, 'Come to me, all you who are weary and burdened, and I will give you rest' (Matt. 11:28).

# Chapter 6: Are Christians free from punishment when they sin?

As we read the Bible, it certainly seems that God often punished, or disciplined, His people for their sins. In Hebrews 12:8 we are told, 'If you are not disciplined (and everyone undergoes discipline), then you are illegitimate children and not true sons.' God's purpose in this is also clear, 'when their uncircumcised hearts are humbled and they pay for their sin, I will remember my covenant' (Lev. 26:41-42). God punished His people for their sins, so that they would return to Him, confessing that they had sinned, and asking for His mercy. An example of this happening is found in 2 Chronicles 12:5-6, where Shishak, king of Egypt, is attacking Jerusalem. God sends the prophet Shemaiah to the leaders of Judah to give them this message from God, 'You have abandoned me; therefore, I now abandon you to Shishak.' The leaders respond by humbling themselves, and saying: 'The LORD is just.' They understood that this was a punishment from God because of their sin.

So we see that God disciplined His people when they sinned, in order that they would confess their sin. This included even people who had not been unfaithful to Him, such as Daniel and Ezra – see their prayers of confession in Daniel 9 and Ezra 9. God didn't only punish His people as a group, He punished individuals, even those very close to Him, such as Moses, who was not allowed to enter the promised land because of his sin (Num. 20:12). Also David was punished for his sin with Bathsheba (2 Sam. 12:10).

Possibly you are thinking that that was in the Old Testament, and that the New Testament is different. If we look at this in more detail, however, we will see that the New Testament agrees with the Old Testament. It is very important to understand this – the Old and New Testaments are in agreement with one another, not against each other.

In the New Testament we also see that God punishes His people when they sin. For example, as Paul writes in 1 Corinthians 11:30, 'That is why many among you are weak and sick, and a number of you have fallen asleep.' The reason given for this was that some were taking part in the Lord's Supper in an unworthy condition. Some people say that Paul is speaking about people who were not really Christians, but it is clear from verse 32 that Paul is speaking to Christians, when he says, 'When we are judged by the Lord, we are being disciplined so that we will not be condemned with the world.' The word translated here as 'disciplined' or 'chastised' is a word which is only used about God's people. We see the same idea in Hebrews 12:6-8: '…the Lord disciplines those he loves, and he punishes everyone he accepts as a son … If you are not disciplined … then you are illegitimate children and not true sons.'

It can be difficult for Christians to accept that God punishes His people. We think like this: 'If I am a Christian, God has forgiven all my sin, so how can He punish me for it? If Jesus was punished for my sin, how can God also punish me? It isn't right for God to do that!' Let me answer like this: Everything God does in the lives of His people is motivated by His love.

His only aim is to do them good, to make them more holy so that they will share in His glory (Heb. 12:10). God never punishes, or disciplines, His children to satisfy His justice. He never punishes us to make us pay in some way for our sins. Jesus Christ has fully satisfied God's justice by His death for us on the cross. All of God's anger at our sin was poured on Jesus, and now we experience God's loving discipline, as He corrects and humbles us. Everything that God does in our lives, He does out of His love for us. His discipline may be unpleasant, just as medicine tastes bitter. But both are for our good, and given to us out of love.

Let me give some reasons why God punishes or disciplines His people:

1. As a warning to wicked people; if God punishes His friends when they sin, what will happen to His enemies? If judgment begins with the house of God, what will happen to those who do not believe the gospel? (1 Pet. 4:17).

2. To show the world that He does what is right. He does not allow His own people to sin and at the same time punish everyone else. There is no favouritism with God.

3. To defend the honour of His name, as in the case of David's sin, 2 Samuel 12:14. When God's own people sin, it is more dishonouring to His name than when unbelievers sin, because we belong to Him.

4. As a warning to other Christians, to keep us from committing the same sins other Christians have committed. Paul talks about this in 1 Corinthians 10:6-12, for example verse 9, 'We should not test the Lord, as some of them did—and were killed by snakes.'

49

5. For our spiritual growth; when we are disciplined by God for our sin, it produces humility in us. It makes us more ready to listen to God, and more willing to avoid sin. God's main aim in all His punishment, or discipline, is to prepare us to share in His glory, as Paul says in 2 Corinthians 4:17, 'For our light and momentary troubles are achieving for us an eternal glory that far outweighs them all.'

As we come to the end of this chapter, I want to say one more thing: not all of God's discipline is because we have sinned. There are times when God disciplines us for other reasons. An example of this is the experience of Job, who was disciplined to test his trust in God, and to prove to the devil that he truly loved God. God may discipline us for the same reason – to test and strengthen our faith. Another example is the apostle Paul, who says that he was given 'a thorn in the flesh' so that he would not *become* proud – not because he was already proud (2 Cor. 12:7). God can discipline us like this, too – so that we will not sin in some way. We can also suffer for doing good, and for preaching the gospel. We must not think that every time God disciplines us, or allows us to go through difficulties, it is because we have sinned.

# Chapter 7: Obedience and freedom

This is the next question we will consider: If Christians have a duty to obey God's moral law, doesn't this limit our freedom? In other words, if we *must* obey God, then how can we say that we are free?

To begin, let me say this: obeying God and being free are not two different things. The reason God saved us was so that we would be free to serve Him, as we clearly see in Luke 1:74-75, 'to rescue us from the hand of our enemies, and to enable us to serve him without fear in holiness and righteousness before him all our days.' Jesus Christ has not saved us from serving God, but He has saved us from serving Him out of fear. He has also saved us from serving other gods, so that we can serve Him, and His 'yoke is easy, and [his] burden is light' (Matt. 11:30).

It is impossible to separate sunshine from the sun, and in the same way it is impossible to separate obedience and salvation. This is what the apostle Paul says in Titus 2:11-12, 'For the grace of God that brings salvation has appeared to all men. It teaches us to say "No" to ungodliness and worldly passions, and to live self-controlled, upright and godly lives in this present age.' So it is absolutely clear that having a duty to obey God is not a denial of our Christian freedom. In fact, without obedience to God, there can be no real freedom.

But what if we don't feel like obeying God? Should we just do something because God tells us to? Isn't it better to wait until we feel like it, or until the Holy Spirit motivates us? Then we will be obeying God freely!

Of course, when the Holy Spirit leads us to do something, it is very important to follow Him. Just like David in 2 Samuel 5:24, when he was at war with the Philistines, and God told him, 'As soon as you hear the sound of marching in the tops of the balsam trees, move quickly, because that will mean the LORD has gone out in front of you to strike the Philistine army.' It is a serious sin to quench the Holy Spirit, so we should respond when He moves our spirits.

But not every influence on our spirits comes from the Holy Spirit. Sometimes Satan will even try to push us into doing some good thing. This may sound very strange, but let me give some examples.

1. When Satan sees a Christian struggling spiritually, then he will try to make that person feel that they should be doing more to serve God – that they should be praying more, and so on. Satan's aim is to make the person even more discouraged and depressed about his or her Christian life.

2. When a Christian is physically weak, then Satan will point out all the things he or she 'should' be doing, because he knows that the person at that moment doesn't have enough strength, and will make themselves weaker by trying to do things.

3. Satan will also push us to try doing something when he thinks we will fail, possibly because the task is very hard. Again, his plan is to discourage us.

4. He will also make it difficult for us to set priorities, to decide what good things we should do – for example, Satan will try to make us so busy doing one good thing, that we don't do other good things that are also important. Or he tries to make us feel guilty about all the things we are not doing, so that we become discouraged.

In all of these examples, Satan often fails because God comes and gives us the strength to serve Him.

This is the difference when the Holy Spirit moves us to do some duty – He also provides the strength we need to do it.

But what if we don't feel the Holy Spirit moving us to do what God has commanded? Let's take the example of prayer. Should we pray even when we don't feel like it? Of course! For one thing, just because we don't *feel* the Holy Spirit at work in us, that doesn't mean that He isn't at work – He may be doing many things in us that we can't feel. Don't forget that God values our obedience when it is a struggle, and not easy for us, and when we need to fight against temptation in order to obey Him.

Also there are many times when we begin praying and our hearts are cold, but as we pray, our hearts are warmed; we start off feeling discouraged, but when we finish praying we are encouraged instead. It is a wonderful fact that often when we begin to do some Christian duty without feeling like doing it, God meets us in the process, and we have a special time of fellowship with Him! This wouldn't ever happen, if we only prayed or did what we should when we felt like it.

We cannot control the Holy Spirit, but we can put ourselves where He is most likely to be found. Just like the paralysed man, who waited at the pool of Bethesda (John 5); he could not control when the Spirit would stir the water, and he couldn't get into the water by himself, but he waited as close to the water as possible – he did what he could, and God met with him and healed him. To use a simple parallel from everyday life, if I want to catch a bus, I need to wait at the bus-stop!

So far we have seen that obeying God's commands is part of our Christian freedom, it is the reason God saved us. We have also seen that we should obey even when we don't feel like it, because God can change our hearts as we obey Him. In the next chapter we will consider in more detail what real Christian obedience is like.

# Chapter 8: Why do we obey God?

In this chapter we will look at what real Biblical obedience is, and how it is different from what we sometimes think of as obedience. To understand this, we must look at the motivation behind obedience, and answer the question, 'Why should we obey God?'

## 1. Wrong answers to the question

### 1. Christians don't obey God to get something from Him.

We are not like servants or employees, who serve their masters so that they will get paid. We are God's children, not employees. We don't have to earn things from our Father. We obey God because what we want most of all is to have a close relationship with Him. We serve God because we enjoy it, not because we need to get something out of it. Because this is true, Christians will serve God even when it doesn't seem to be 'worth it'; to be serving God is a reward in itself. We don't obey God in order to get to heaven, or to get any blessings from God. We know that nothing we do can get us to heaven, or can deserve God's blessing. We rely totally on Jesus Christ, and what He has done for us. We depend on Him completely, and not at all on our obedience.

## *2. Christians don't obey God out of fear of punishment, or to have a problem-free life.*

There are many people who do good things because they are afraid of what will happen to them if they don't. They don't want to stop sinning, but they don't want to go to hell either, so they change their behaviour. It's like a businessman on a ship that is sinking – to save his own life he will throw all his goods into the sea, but only because it's absolutely necessary. Obviously, he doesn't have any real desire to do it! There are many people who do good things without any desire to do them, just because they think they must if they want to get to heaven. They may stop doing some particular sin, but only because they are afraid of the consequences if they don't. In their hearts they still love the sin, and wish they could do it and get away with it.

For Christians it's very different; they don't think of obedience as something very unpleasant that just has to be done (rather like taking medicine). Instead they see obedience as something desirable, because it pleases God and gives them a closer relationship with Him. Christians don't get pleasure any more from sinning. They see sin as a terrible thing, a poison which they want to avoid. For them the worst punishment would be to lose this close relationship with God. They want to please God. They would obey God even if dis-obedience wasn't punished.

## *3. Christians don't obey God to get a clear conscience.*

Many people only do good things because they want to feel good, that is, they want their conscience to be at peace. When this is a person's reason for doing good things, they don't actually enjoy what they are doing. Their heart isn't really in it, it's just a duty. Conscience can show us what is right and wrong, just like a signpost can show us the way we should go. But it can't give us the desire or strength to do what we should.

## 2. The true reason why Christians obey God

Because it is who they are! Christians enjoy obeying God and take pleasure in doing what God wants because their hearts have been changed. They have a new nature, and this new nature *wants* to obey God's commands. Christians have new desires, which come from their new nature, and this makes them *want* to do what is right – they enjoy it! This enjoyment is a sign of a true Christian. Real obedience comes from the heart, and includes the desire to obey.

This is obvious if we think about the command to love God, for example. It's not possible to love someone without our hearts being involved. A Christian doesn't love God just because there is a command to love Him; he loves God because he sees that God is worthy to be loved, that God is wonderful and beautiful. A real Christian would still love God even if he wasn't commanded to do it.

Or let's take the example of prayer again. A real Christian prays, not because God commands us to pray (although it is true that he does), but because he wants to have fellowship with God. It is a pleasure to him to pray (although as we have seen, sometimes it is difficult); he wants to talk to his Father, and enjoy time with Him, and he knows that prayer is a wonderful privilege. So also in this case, a real Christian would still pray even if God hadn't commanded it.

It's like this: a healthy person doesn't eat just because he must, he eats because he wants to! He has a healthy appetite, he feels like eating, and he enjoys his food. That's what a Christian is like when it comes to obeying God. He does it not just because he must, but because he has the appetite to do it. He obeys God because he wants to – he enjoys it!

Our eyes see without being forced to; it is what eyes do naturally. It's the same with our new nature – it is natural for it to obey God. God's grace is active in us, motivating us to obey His commands. This is why a believer enjoys obeying God: obedience comes naturally, out of his new heart. As the Psalm writer says in Psalm 40:8, 'I *delight* to do Your will, O my God' (NKJV emphasis added). Why? The Psalm writer goes on to tell us, 'Your law is within my heart'.

God promised to write His law on our hearts (Jer. 31:33; Ezek. 36:26-27). This means that God will put His law into us, so that it becomes part of who we are. Then obedience to God's law becomes natural, coming from the heart itself, and giving us pleasure. This is what we read about in Psalm 119. To take just one verse, look at verse 32, 'I run in the path of your commands, for you have set my heart free.'

Of course we don't always naturally want to obey God. There are times when obedience seems difficult and we don't have any desire to obey. This means that there is something wrong with our spiritual health. It's like a person who is sick; they will eat because they know they must if they want to get well, but they don't have any appetite. They force themselves to eat because if they don't, they will die. Or to use the example of the eye again – if our eyes are painful, and it's hard to use them, that means there's something wrong with the eye. A healthy eye doesn't find it difficult to see.

If Christians don't want to obey God, then there is something wrong spiritually. It could be that we have started to love someone or something else more than God Himself. It could be that we have fallen into some sin. It could be our old sinful nature trying to get back in control. It could be that we are going through a time of great difficulty or temptation. But even at times like this, when a believer is at his lowest point spiritually, he still has more of a heart for God than an unbeliever at his highest point. This is because he still has a new heart and a new nature, and the unbeliever does not.

So in this chapter we have seen that real Christian freedom means that we obey God's commands because we want to, and we enjoy doing what God has commanded.

# Chapter 9: Obedience and rewards

The question we will answer in this chapter is this: If real Christian obedience means obeying God freely, from the heart, can we at the same time obey Him in order to get some reward? Or we could ask the question this way: If I am obeying God to get something from Him, then aren't my motives wrong?

Before we start to answer this question, let me make one thing absolutely clear: we can never earn salvation. We don't do good works in order to deserve God's forgiveness and get a place in heaven. The Bible is absolutely clear that salvation can only be received as a gracious gift (Titus 3:5; Rom. 6:23).

So now we can begin to discuss the question. Should we be motivated by rewards to obey God? There are two points of view on the subject. One view is that we shouldn't be thinking about rewards at all. Those who take this view say that if you are thinking about rewards, then you are obeying God in order to get something from Him, and not because you freely want to obey Him. They also say that God has already graciously given us everything in Christ, so we cannot do anything ourselves to get anything from God.

The other view is that God Himself gives us rewards as a motivation for obedience, so it can't be wrong for us to think about them. Here are some Bible verses which suggest this:

- 'For if you live according to the sinful nature, you will die; but if by the Spirit you put to death the misdeeds of the body, you will live' (Rom. 8:13).

- 'Give yourselves fully to the work of the Lord, because you know that your labour in the Lord is not in vain' (1 Cor. 15:58).

- 'So then, dear friends, since you are looking forward to this, make every effort to be found spotless, blameless and at peace with him' (2 Pet. 3:14; see also 2 Pet. 1:5-12).

- 'Let us not become weary in doing good, for at the proper time we will reap a harvest if we do not give up' (Gal. 6:9).

We also have the example of godly people in the Bible, who were motivated to obey God by rewards. A clear example of this is Moses, as the writer to the Hebrews tells us, 'He chose to be ill-treated along with the people of God rather than to enjoy the pleasures of sin for a short time. He regarded disgrace for the sake of Christ as of greater value than the treasures of Egypt, because he was looking ahead to his reward' (Heb. 11:25-26).

Another example (from the New Testament) is that of the apostle Paul, who says these words, 'One thing I do: Forgetting what is behind and straining towards what is ahead, I press on towards the goal to win the prize for which God has called me heavenwards in Christ Jesus' (Phil. 3:13-14).

So which is the correct view?

Firstly, we need to understand what kind of rewards we are talking about. Rewards in the Bible can be divided into different categories: material (that is, rewards we receive only in this life, such as health, riches, success, and so on), spiritual (for example, justification, victory over lust, joy, peace, etc.)

and eternal (heaven, glory, eternal life, freedom from sin, and so on).

I want us to look at each category in turn, beginning with material blessings.

## 1. Material Blessings

Should a true Christian serve God in order to receive the good things of this life? A non-Christian can obey God for that reason; he wants good things, and he thinks that serving God is the way to get them. Of course, such a person is only really serving himself, not God. If he doesn't get what he thinks God should give him, then he stops serving God. We see this in the gospels, where some people followed Jesus because He had miraculously fed them (John 6:26), and after this many of them stopped following Him. Another example is in Hosea, where God says that the people want His blessings, but do not want Him, 'They do not cry out to me from their hearts but wail upon their beds. They gather together for grain and new wine but turn away from me' (Hosea 7:14).

A true Christian won't serve God like that. For him, the main reasons to obey God are because God has commanded him to do so, and because God has been so good to him. He is now a new creation in Christ, and this gives him the strength and desire to obey God.

The good things of this life are not as important to a Christian as pleasing God. This is his real motivation to serve God. The temporal blessings of this life are unimportant when compared to spiritual matters. They cannot be a powerful enough motivation to obey God; if they play any part, it is just like the oil that greases an engine, but doesn't give power and direction to it. We must never make the blessings of this life the main reason for our obedience.

It is also important to understand the difference between the old and new covenants. In Deuteronomy 28:1-14 we read of the temporal blessings for obedience which God promised to His people. We need to see that these blessings were never the main reason the people were given for obeying God. These blessings were incentives, and were designed to make obedience attractive to the people. God's people at that time did not have the fullness of His Holy Spirit, as we now do in the new covenant. God was dealing with His people then as under-age children, with the law as their school master, as Paul says in Galatians 3:24-25, 'So the law was put in charge to lead us to Christ ... now that faith has come, we are no longer under the supervision of the law.'

Now, under the Gospel, we do not have the same promises of temporal blessings if we obey God. In fact, we should expect hardships and suffering in this life, just as Jesus said to the apostles:

- 'All men will hate you because of me' (Matt. 10:22).

- 'A time is coming when anyone who kills you will think he is offering a service to God' (John 16:2).

Hardships and difficulties will come into the life of every Christian:

- 'Everyone who wants to live a godly life in Christ Jesus will be persecuted' (2 Tim. 3:12).

- 'We must go through many hardships to enter the kingdom of God' (Acts 14:22).

- 'If anyone would come after me, he must deny himself and take up his cross daily and follow me' (Luke 9:23).

It should be obvious from all these verses that Christians are not promised only good things in this life (as the world understands good things). We have instead the promise of Jeremiah 32:40, 'I will make an everlasting covenant with them: I will never stop doing good to them, and I will inspire them to fear me, so that they will never turn away from me.'

God promises that He will never stop doing us good, but we need to understand that this 'good' does not necessarily mean the good things of this life. In fact, God may work in our lives in such a way that our losses may actually be blessings, and so-called 'good things' may be punishments. The promise of temporal good things, such as riches and prosperity, does not belong to a believer in the gospel. In the gospel we are promised mercy and spiritual blessings. God is now working *all* things for our good:

'And we know that in all things God works for the good of those who love him, who have been called according to his purpose' (Rom. 8:28).

So in answer to the question 'Should a Christian obey God in order to receive temporal rewards?' I say this: it is much better to obey because of the blessings we have already received in the gospel, than in the hope of getting some other good thing from God.

It is better to see it like this: we don't obey so that God will give us this or that good thing, we obey because we believe that God will bless us, both in this life, and in eternity. God's promises to us say that, and we obey because we believe Him:

'Since we have these promises, dear friends, let us purify ourselves from everything that contaminates body and spirit, perfecting holiness out of reverence for God' (2 Cor. 7:1).

'Whatever you do, work at it with all your heart, as working for the Lord, not for men, since you know that you will receive an inheritance from the Lord as a reward' (Col. 3:23-24).

We already have God's promises of blessing: these promises are certain, and they motivate us to live for God in this present life.

## 2. Spiritual Blessings

By spiritual blessings I mean anything we would consider as a spiritual benefit, such as joy, peace, assurance, and so on. Should we be motivated to obey God's commands in order to receive such blessings? Isn't it true that Jesus has already obtained all these blessings for us by His obedience?

We need to answer those questions in the following way: Jesus has obtained all God's blessings for us, that is true. But God has also defined the way, or the means, by which we receive those blessings. For example, Jesus says in Matthew 7:7, 'Ask and it will be given to you.' In this verse we see that the way to receive is by asking. In Revelation 21:6 we read these words, 'To him who is thirsty I will give to drink without cost from the spring of the water of life.' In order to receive this living water, a person needs to recognize that they are thirsty – that's the condition attached to God's promise of living water.

This leads us to another very important point: God graciously gives us whatever we need, so that we can receive His blessings. He gives us faith so that we can ask, and therefore receive. He causes us to be spiritually thirsty, so that then He can satisfy us with the water of life. We never earn or deserve God's spiritual blessings. God gives them to us out of His grace.

## 3. Eternal Blessings (or Rewards)

Firstly let's be clear that we don't earn eternal life, or heaven, by our obedience here on earth. As it says clearly in Titus 3:5, 'He saved us, not because of righteous things we had done, but because of his mercy.'

It is also true, however, that our obedience to God during our time on earth is important. God is making us ready for heaven, and before He takes us to be with Him, He begins to make us more like Himself. As we try to obey God, we can be encouraged when we think of what is waiting for us in the future. This is not at all the same thing as trying to earn heaven by our good works.

Very often, especially when a person has not been a Christian very long, he or she is motivated by the desire to escape hell, and get to heaven instead. For new believers this is normal, but as they begin to see more of the beauty and goodness of God, then they want to serve Him more for Himself, because He deserves it. Fear of hell can make a person turn to God, but once a person has tasted God's mercy, then he wants to serve God with everything he is and has. He isn't thinking, 'What will God give me if I serve him?' He's thinking instead, 'What can I give to God?'

So should we think about heaven and glory to motivate us to obey God? Some people say no, because they think that means obeying God in order to get eternal happiness, which is just using God to get something from Him. Such people have this problem: they have a wrong understanding about heaven. Let me explain: many people have a wrong *idea* about heaven. Worldly people imagine heaven to be a place of constant enjoyment, as they define enjoyment – riches, feasting, no more problems, etc. Certainly the Bible does describe heaven in terms that we can understand – golden streets, precious jewels, and so on. But we mustn't take this literally, as heaven is far more wonderful than that! God is using these pictures to give us some small understanding of heaven. God doesn't need gold or jewels to make heaven glorious – next to His glory, the most beautiful treasures of the world are nothing! What makes heaven glorious is the presence of God Himself. If we understand this, then there's nothing wrong with thinking about heaven to motivate us to obedience here on earth.

What are the rewards we will have in heaven? The greatest reward heaven will give the Christian is to enjoy the presence of God – Father, Son and Holy Spirit – in a far deeper way than we can know in this life, and to be with God forever. The rewards of heaven are these: enjoying the presence of God, the Father, Son and Spirit, and resting forever in Him. Our obedience *must* be motivated by our desire to enjoy the presence of God! As David says in Psalm 73:25, 'Whom have I in heaven but you? And earth has nothing I desire besides you.'

This is how Moses was thinking when he gave up all the riches of Egypt – the glories of heaven were much more precious to him, and by comparison, the world couldn't offer him anything that came close to the reward that waited for him. This is also what the apostle Paul says, 'Our light and momentary troubles are achieving for us an eternal glory that far outweighs them all. So we fix our eyes not on what is seen, but on what is unseen' (2 Cor. 4:17-18).

Thinking Biblically about heaven will make a great difference to how you live your Christian life. Here are just some examples:

*Thankfulness*

If we think about what is waiting for us in heaven, we will be thankful people, often praising God, as Peter does in 1 Peter 1:3, 'Praise be to the God and Father of our Lord Jesus Christ! In his great mercy he has given us new birth into a living hope … into an inheritance that can never perish, spoil or fade – kept in heaven for you.'

*Joyfulness*

Thinking of heaven, we can be filled with joy even when we are going through great difficulties, like those Christians we read about in Hebrews 10:34, 'You … joyfully accepted the confiscation of your property, because you knew that you yourselves had better and lasting possessions.' No matter how difficult our lives might be now, our certain hope for the future can give us joy.

*Strength to serve God*

Our future hope enables us to keep serving God now, in all circumstances. 'Whatever you do, work at it with all your heart, as working for the Lord, not for men, since you know that you will receive an inheritance from the Lord as a reward' (Col. 3:23-24).

*Submission to God's will*

We can be content with whatever God sends us. We can be content if we are poor here on earth, because we know that one day we will be rich. We can be content though despised here, because one day we will be honoured. We can go through all kinds of difficulties, because we know we will be comforted. We can be imprisoned, because one day we will be perfectly free. We can lose everything, because one day we will have everything. God will be more to us than what we have lost, and that will be forever. We can welcome trials, sorrows and difficulties, because we know that after sorrow comes joy, and after trial comes rest. Even death itself is only the beginning of eternal life, and our enjoyment of the great and glorious things that God has prepared for us.

## Chapter 10: Can those set free by Christ become slaves to sin again?

Let us remind ourselves of what it means to be a slave to sin, as the Bible sees it. Being a slave to sin means being under the control of sin, and of Satan, and under the curse and impossible demands of the law. We looked at this in detail in chapter 1, and we saw that Christians have been set free from all these things.

It is absolutely clear that a Christian cannot go back to being under the control of sin and Satan, and under the curse of the law. Look at Romans 6:14, 'For sin shall not be your master, because you are not under law, but under grace.' A person who has been made free by Christ cannot become Satan's slave again; this verse promises him that. There will still be times when sin will have a victory in the Christian's life, and may even capture him, as Paul says in Romans 7:23. But the Christian is never a willing prisoner to sin or Satan; he doesn't happily surrender to sin. He may fall into specific sins, but he will never again become the contented servant of sin and Satan.

It is also impossible for a Christian to go back to being under the curse of the law. The law cannot condemn the Christian, because he is not under law, but under grace. It is impossible for a Christian to put himself outside the grace of

God, and so he cannot go back to being under the curse and demands of the law.

However, sin does affect the Christian. Even though he can't become a slave again to sin, his freedom can be spoiled by his sin. I don't really like to use this phrase, but we could call this 'partial' or 'limited' slavery. There are two ways that a Christian's sin affects his freedom in Christ.

## 1. Loss of peace and joy

Sin causes a Christian to lose his sense of peace and joy. This is what happened to David when he sinned, and in Psalm 51 he prays, 'Restore to me the joy of your salvation' (v. 12). David had not lost his salvation, but he had lost his sense of joy.

Sin spoils the close relationship that Christians have with God; when we sin we no longer have a clean conscience, and we cannot clearly see God's grace at work in us.

God's promises of grace do not depend on anything we do. They are absolutely unconditional, and never change. God's promises of peace, joy and comfort are conditional – they depend on how we live. We do not *earn* peace and joy by our obedience, but as we obey we will have peace and joy; they are the 'side-effects' of obedience. We cannot expect to have joy and peace if we are sinning. Here are some verses which show this:

- 'The fruit of righteousness will be peace' (Isa. 32:17).
- 'You come to the help of those who gladly do right' (Isa. 64:5).
- 'Great peace have they who love your law' (Ps. 119:165).
- 'Whoever has my commands and obeys them, he is the one who loves me. He who loves me will be loved by my Father, and I too will love him and show myself to him' (John 14:21).

So if we don't walk in obedience, we may expect to lose our sense of peace and joy. If we do not follow the Holy Spirit's commands, we will lose the peace and joy He gives. In Isaiah 59:2 we read this, 'Your iniquities have separated you from your God; your sins have hidden his face from you, so that he will not hear.' This is not a complete or final separation, but a Christian's sin creates a distance between God and himself.

We may also expect all kinds of spiritual trouble. We cannot lose our salvation, but we can lose our assurance or confidence that we are saved, we can lose the evidence that shows us we are saved, and get to the point where we even forget that we are saved. Peter describes a person like this in 2 Peter 1:9, 'He is short-sighted and blind, and has forgotten that he has been cleansed from his past sins.'

So what can we do when we have sinned? Firstly, we must remind ourselves that our sins do not change the fact that God has forgiven us, and that we are saved. Then we must believe that God is full of mercy, and that there is enough grace in Jesus to deal with all our sin. We can be encouraged – God has shown us our sin because He wants us to repent, to come back to Him and have peace and joy again! Our peace and joy depend on Jesus Christ and His obedience, not ours. Jesus gives us peace, as He says in John 16:33, 'I have told you these things, so that in me you may have peace.' The foundation of a Christian's peace is what Jesus Christ has done for him, but this peace is fed and grows, nurtured by obedience.

## 2. Loss of pleasure in serving God

Sin also affects our Christian service, so that serving God is no longer a pleasure, as it used to be. When we have lost our sense of joy and peace, serving God becomes more like a duty than a delight. After he sinned, David asked God to 'grant me a willing spirit' (Ps. 51:12). He had lost the willing spirit he had before he sinned. Sin cannot make a Christian a slave again, but it can stop him from serving God freely as a son. He still prays, for example, but he doesn't have the sense of enjoying fellowship with God that he used to have in prayer. He does what he knows is right, but it isn't enjoyable any more, just like a sick person may eat, but has no appetite to enjoy his food (as we saw in chapter 8).

So Christians do have much to lose by sinning, although they cannot become slaves again to sin.

# Chapter 11: Conclusion

## 1. A Word to Non-Christians

If it is true, as I have said earlier in this book, that only Jesus can set us free, then if you are not a Christian you are in a terrifying position.

If you are not a Christian, then you are still a slave to sin. Sin is your master, and you are happy to be its servant. You don't want to be free, because you enjoy serving sin. You may have heard the gospel message many times, but you still choose to serve sin. You are an active partner in this slavery – your desires keep you constantly working, trying to satisfy them. You are ready to sacrifice your time, money and energy to satisfy your desires, but you won't give up anything to have God.

This is a terrible position to be in, because we are talking about spiritual slavery – your soul is not free. Any kind of slavery is an awful thing, but spiritual slavery is the worst of all. One of the worst things about it is that you can't see it. You are a slave, but you don't realise it. You don't feel like a slave, and you may even think that you are free. The most serious illnesses are those where the patient is unconscious, and it's the same with our spiritual condition. To have a dead conscience is far worse than having a conscience which feels guilty.

You are powerless to change your condition. You cannot stop being a slave to sin, and no-one else can help you to free yourself. Only Jesus Christ can free people from slavery to sin, because the price of freedom is so high. You have no strength to free yourself (Rom. 5:6-8). It's like being stuck in sinking sand – the more you struggle to get out, the deeper you sink into the sand. This is truly a terrible condition to be in.

But that's not all! You are also a slave to Satan. You are a prisoner, and Satan is the prison governor. You can only do what he allows you to do. He is a cruel governor, never kind or merciful. He keeps some of his prisoners locked up, completely under the control of their desires or addictions. He allows other prisoners to walk around in the prison yard, but whenever he likes, Satan can lock them up inside again, because he has control over them. They are no more free than the prisoners who never leave their cells.

All of us are born in this prison. We are all born as slaves. No part of us is free – our minds, our wills, our consciences, our desires – every part of us – is in slavery to Satan. We cannot do a single thing freely. Even when we do the same things that free people do, we are doing them in a spirit of slavery. For example, we can pray, but we will be praying as slaves, not as children. We can do good things, but we do them because we're afraid of punishment, not because we love God. Our spirits are in slavery, so everything we do, we do as slaves.

As well as this, you are a slave to the law of God. You are under a curse, because you cannot keep this law (Gal. 3:10). This means that everything concerning you is cursed, even the 'good things' you may be enjoying here and now. You cannot escape this curse. Every human being ever born, except for Jesus Christ, has been born under the curse of God.

You are a slave to the impossible demands of God's law. If you look at what God's law requires of you, you will see that you cannot keep it (Acts 15:10). God's law demands perfect obedience, all the time, as we see in James 2:10, 'For whoever keeps the whole law and yet stumbles at just one point is guilty of breaking all of it.' God's law won't accept our best efforts or intentions, we must achieve perfection. If we don't achieve perfection, how hard we have tried makes no difference.

You must keep all the law perfectly. It's not enough to be very good at keeping some parts of God's law, or to keep all of God's law most of the time. The smallest failure means total failure. One sin, and you are condemned. There's no forgiveness, no second chance, no opportunity to make up for your failure. The law doesn't accept repentance.

This is your terrible condition if you are not a Christian.

## 2. A Word to Christians

As we remember how terrible our condition was before Jesus freed us from sin, we should be more and more thankful for the wonderful privilege of freedom we now have. Our freedom is a precious thing, and like all precious things, we need to be careful with it. Firstly, we can misuse our freedom. Let me explain how we can do this:

- When we harm the faith of other Christians. In the church at Corinth there were some young Christians who were eating food offered to idols, just to show that they were free to do so. The apostle Paul says to them, '"Everything is permissible" – but not everything is beneficial. "Everything is permissible" – but not everything is constructive. Nobody should seek his own good, but the good of others' (1 Cor. 10:23-24). We are not to display our freedom in such a way that another Christian's faith is harmed (see 1 Cor. 8:7-13).

- When we decide that we don't have to obey God's Word. As I have already shown, this is actually slavery to sin. Real Christian freedom means obeying God, as Peter makes clear, 'Live as free

77

men, but do not use your freedom as a cover-up for evil; live as servants of God' (1 Pet. 2:16).

- When we make our own judgments about what is right and wrong. Christian freedom has rules and limits. We are not free to simply please ourselves, 'You, my brothers, were called to be free. But do not use your freedom to indulge the sinful nature; rather, serve one another in love' (Gal. 5:13).

Secondly, we must protect our freedom, as Paul says, 'It is for freedom that Christ has set us free. Stand firm, then, and do not let yourselves be burdened again by a yoke of slavery' (Gal. 5:1).

- We must not allow any other person to rule over our conscience, and we should not obey anyone, in the absolute sense in which we obey Jesus Christ. Even the best people can be wrong sometimes, and so we must test everything by God's Word, and not allow anyone to have complete authority over our lives, apart from God Himself.

- We must not try to justify ourselves by keeping God's law. Even as Christians, we often want to earn our salvation (or at least contribute something to it) by our good works and obedience. God, however, gives us salvation as a free gift! Our works have nothing to do with it, and we must not forget this. Christians can easily start to expect things from God because of what they do, rather than because of God's grace. This makes us proud of ourselves when we are doing well, and when we fail, we do not go to Jesus for help and forgiveness, as we should. We must learn to depend completely on Christ, no matter how well or badly we are doing. We need to live like people who expect nothing from the law – neither condemnation nor justification, neither punishment nor praise. It isn't easy to live like this, above the law, and at the same time obeying it, but that is what Christian freedom means.

Grace
Publications

## Grace Publications Trust

Grace Publication Trust is a not for profit organisation that exists to glorify God by making the truth of God's Word (as declared in the Baptist Confessions of 1689 and 1966) clear and understandable, so that:

- Christians will be helped to preach Christ
- Christians will know Christ better and delight in him more
- Christians will be equipped to live for Christ
- Seekers will come to know Christ

From its beginning in the late 1970s the Trust has published simplified and modernised versions of important Christian books written earlier, for example by some of the Reformers and Puritans. These books have helped introduce the riches of the past to a new generation and have proved particularly useful in parts of Asia and Africa where English is widely spoken as a second language. These books are now appearing in editions co-published with Christian Focus as *Grace Essentials*.

More details of the Trust's work can be found on the web site at *http://www.gracepublications.co.uk*.

# Christian Focus Publications

Our mission statement –

STAYING FAITHFUL

In dependence upon God we seek to impact the world through literature faithful to His infallible Word, the Bible. Our aim is to ensure that the Lord Jesus Christ is presented as the only hope to obtain forgiveness of sin, live a useful life and look forward to heaven with Him.

Our books are published in four imprints:

### CHRISTIAN
## FOCUS

Popular works including biographies, commentaries, basic doctrine and Christian living.

### CHRISTIAN
## HERITAGE

Books representing some of the best material from the rich heritage of the church.

## MENTOR

Books written at a level suitable for Bible College and seminary students, pastors, and other serious readers. The imprint includes commentaries, doctrinal studies, examination of current issues and church history.

## CF4•K

Children's books for quality Bible teaching and for all age groups: Sunday school curriculum, puzzle and activity books; personal and family devotional titles, biographies and inspirational stories – because you are never too young to know Jesus!

Christian Focus Publications Ltd,
Geanies House, Fearn, Ross-shire,
IV20 1TW, Scotland, United Kingdom.
www.christianfocus.com